Discovering
Cultures

Mexico

Sandy Asher

BENCHMARK **B**OOKS

MARSHALL CAVENDISH
NEW YORK

With thanks to Dr. Ray Sadler, Department of History, New Mexico State University, Las Cruces, New Mexico, for the careful review of this manuscript.

Acknowledgments

My thanks to the following people for their generous help: Ben Asher, Edgar Bueno Hernández, Yolanda Lorge, Dr. Jorge Padron, Karla Paniagua, and Emily Thompson. *Gracias!*

Benchmark Books
Marshall Cavendish
99 White Plains Road, Tarrytown, New York 10591-9001
Text copyright © 2003 by Marshall Cavendish Corporation
Map and illustrations copyright © 2003 by Marshall Cavendish Corporation
Map and illustrations by Salvatore Murdocca
Book design by Virginia Pope

Library of Congress Cataloging-in-Publication Data

Asher, Sandy.
Mexico / by Sandy Asher.
p. cm. — (Discovering cultures)
Includes bibliographical references and index.
Summary: An introduction to Mexico, highlighting the country's geography, people, foods, schools, recreation, celebrations, and language.
ISBN 0-7614-1175-5
1. Mexico—Juvenile literature. [1. Mexico.] I. Title. II. Series.
F1208.5 .A84 2002
972—dc21   2001007460

Photo Research by Candlepants Incorporated
Cover Photo: Getty Creative / Stone / Cosmo Condino

The photographs in this book are used by permission and through the courtesy of; Getty Creative: Stone / David Hiser, 1; Stone / Mark Lewis, 6; Photodisc / Duncan Smith, 15; Stone / Robert Frerck, 21 (top); FPG International / Bryan Peterson, 24; The Image Bank / Rubens Neves da Rocha Fiho, 34. Corbis: Dave G. Houser, 4-5; AFP, 8, 40, 45 (top); Danny Lehman, 9, 16, 19, 25, 32; Kevin Schafer, 10; Michael and Patricia Fogden, 11; Charles and Josetts Lenars, 13; Macduff Everton, 17, back cover; Richard Glover, 20; Nik Wheeler, 22, 39; Jan Butchofsky-Houser, 26; Carl and Ann Purcell, 27; Phil Schermeister, 28; Karl Weatherly, 30; Reuters NewMedia, Inc, 31; Sergio Dorantes, 36-37; Kelly-Mooney Photography, 41; Bettmann, 45 (bottom). Cory Langley: 12, 21(bottom), 33; Art Resource, NY: Schalkwijk, 14. Art Archive: 38. Center for Creative Photography, University of Arizona: 44.

Cover: *Mayan pyramid*; Title page: *Quetzal dancer in Aztec dress*

Printed in Hong Kong

1 3 5 6 4 2

Turn the Pages...

¡Hola!

Every year, people from around the world travel to Mexico and are greeted by this Spanish word for hello.

Visitors enjoy the warmth of Mexico's sunshine and its people. But what is it like to live there—not just on vacation, but every day?

Girls dressed for a Cinco de Mayo celebration

Where in the World Is Mexico?

Mexico sits just across the Rio Grande from the state of Texas. It is the southernmost country in North America.

Long and narrow, Mexico forms a graceful curve between the United States to the north and Guatemala and Belize to the south. To the west is the Pacific Ocean. The Gulf of Mexico and the Caribbean Sea lie to the east.

Two huge mountain ranges run the length of the country, forming a giant V. These are the Eastern and Western Sierra Madre Mountains. Most Mexicans live between these mountain ranges, in an area called the Mexican Plateau. Many of them live in or near the capital, Mexico City. This busy, modern city is home to almost 22 million people.

Skyscrapers tower above modern Mexico City

Baja California

Western
Sierra
Madre
Mountains

Río Grande

Eastern
Sierra
Madre
Mountains

Mexican Plateau

Gulf of Mexico

Pacific
Ocean

Mexico City

Mount Popocatépetl

Yucatan Peninsula

Caribbean
Sea

N

NW   NE

W   E

SW   SE

S

Mount Popocatépetl blows smoke and ash into the sky.

Earthquakes and volcanoes have shaped much of Mexico's hilly land. Mount Popocatépetl, near the capital, is one of the country's highest volcanoes. Its name means smoking mountain in Nahuatl, an ancient Aztec language. Mount Popocatépetl is old but still active. Now and then, it shoots hot ash high into the air.

Palm trees on the beach

Famous for its sunny beaches and the mild climate of its high plateau, Mexico often surprises visitors with its snow-covered mountain peaks. Northern areas of the plateau tend to be dry and cold in the winter. Unable to grow many crops, farmers in the north raise cattle.

Areas in the southern plateau enjoy a longer rainy season. The soil there is very fertile. Farmers grow corn, cotton, fruit, wheat, barley, and beans.

Tropical rain forests, swamps, and lagoons are found in the southern lowlands and on the Yucatán Peninsula. Because of their bright sunshine and high humidity, these sea-level areas are known as *tierra caliente* (hot land).

To the west lies Baja California. It stretches south like a long, thin finger into the Pacific Ocean below Mexico's border with the United States. Baja California is mostly hot, dry desert. More than 120 kinds of cactuses grow on this peninsula.

In addition to its many crops and exotic plants and animals, Mexico is rich in oil, natural gas, and minerals. Some of its mines produce silver, gold, copper, and lead.

With its mountains, beaches, rain forests, and deserts, Mexico is truly a varied land!

Many different kinds of cactuses grow in Baja California.

The Quetzal

The quetzal is one of many colorful birds that live in the rain forests of Mexico. It is about the size of a pigeon, with a long tail and bright green, gold, red, and white feathers. The quetzal is hard to spot in its forest habitat. People even have wondered if this famous bird really exists.

The quetzal has had a long history. The ancient Mayan and Aztec peoples honored it as a symbol of freedom and wealth. They believed that the quetzal would die if it were captured. They also treasured its beautiful feathers. They caught the birds to pluck their tail feathers, and then set them free to grow more. People wore fancy headdresses made with the quetzal's feathers in religious ceremonies.

Today, this highly valued bird is in great danger. Poachers now hunt and kill the quetzal for its feathers. And as rain forests are cut down to make way for farmland, this shy bird is losing its habitat. Mexicans and others who admire the quetzal for its beauty and its important place in history hope to preserve it for future generations.

What Makes Mexico Mexican?

The people of modern Mexico are as varied as their land. Some can trace their families directly back to Aztec, Mayan, or Spanish ancestors. But most are *mestizos*, a blend of both native and Spanish peoples that is uniquely Mexican.

Mexico's official name is Los Estados Unidos Mexicanos (The United Mexican States). Like the United States of America, Mexico is a democracy. Its citizens vote for a president and for the governors who lead its thirty-one states.

Spanish is Mexico's national language. The early Spanish explorers introduced it in the 1500s. The language is spoken a little differently in the two countries, but people from Mexico and Spain can understand one another

The people of Mexico are part of a rich culture.

A man in traditional native clothes

very well. Along with their language, the Spanish brought the Catholic religion to Mexico. Today, most Mexicans attend a Catholic church.

Many Mexicans carry on customs handed down from their native ancestors. In rural towns and villages, people may speak Mayan, Zapotec, Nahuatl, or another native language in addition to Spanish. Local dress, foods, and celebrations reflect an area's special heritage.

The music and folk dances of Mexico are world famous. The first *mariachis* began playing there in the eighteenth century. Today, the lively sound of their guitars, violins, trumpets, and singers can be heard at *fiestas*, in restaurants, and on the plazas of Mexico's cities. The Ballet Folklórico de México (Folklore Ballet of Mexico) travels the world to share the country's music and dance. At home, they perform at the one-hundred-year-old Bellas Artes (Fine Arts) theater in Mexico City.

Museums in Mexico and around the world display the work of Mexican artists. Among the most famous is Diego Rivera, who is best known for his murals—large paintings that cover entire walls. These murals often show scenes from Mexico's history. Their bold images decorate government buildings as well as museums.

People from the United States and Mexico often cross the border between their countries on business or vacation. Many Mexican-Americans who live in the United States still have relatives in Mexico. So it is not surprising that these neighboring countries have many things in common.

In the southwestern United States, the styles of many buildings show a strong Mexican influence. Mexicans

Our Bread *painted by Diego Rivera*

also gave Spanish names to several states and many cities in this area, including San Francisco and Santa Fe. That's because Texas, Arizona, New Mexico, California, and parts of Nevada, Utah, and Colorado belonged to Mexico before the Mexican-American War of 1846–1848.

Do you know someone with a pet Chihuahua? This small dog dates back to the days of the Aztec Empire in Mexico. It takes its name from Mexico's biggest state, Chihuahua.

Which is your favorite, vanilla or chocolate? Both come from Mexico, where they have been adding flavor to menus for hundreds of years. Peanuts, chewing gum, and poinsettias—the bright red Christmas flower—also have their origins in Mexico.

The tiny Chihuahua is named after Mexico's largest state.

Corn, beans, chili peppers, and tomatoes were all brought north from Mexico. You have probably tasted them in Mexican dishes, such as tacos, burritos, tortillas, and salsa. In the United States, these are often prepared in a style known as Tex-Mex, a blend of Texan and Mexican foods.

Handmade crafts have been an important part of Mexican life since ancient times. Visitors often bring home fine silver jewelry, colorful pottery, and handwoven wool blankets and shawls as souvenirs.

Mexican artisans create hand-painted pottery.

Traditional Dress

On an ordinary workday in Mexico's busy cities, most people wear the same kinds of clothes that you see in the United States. But each Mexican state also has its own traditional dress, which is worn at *fiestas*, weddings, and religious ceremonies.

In rural areas, everyday clothes may be handmade. Often, children learn to weave and decorate cloth just as their ancestors did hundreds of years ago. They use natural dyes and local materials, such as wool and cotton.

In the villages of Chiápas, a state in southern Mexico, women weave outdoors. Like their Mayan ancestors, they use backstrap looms. One end of the loom is tied to a tree. The weaver leans forward and back against a waist belt to keep the threads straight and tight.

The cloth is then made into tunics for men and *huipili* for women, the traditional dress worn in Chiápas for centuries. Colored yarn is woven into the cloth to create flowers and other designs. These patterns, like the looms themselves, have been handed down from one generation to another.

Living in Mexico

For much of Mexico's history, small villages dotted the countryside. Families lived and worked on farms around each village. The village was a central place to shop, attend church, and visit with neighbors.

People still work the land in rural areas of Mexico, but most of them are poor. Few people own enough land to make a living at farming. Many families live in one-room houses. Children help with chores, tend crops, and care for their families' chickens, goats, or pigs.

Some houses in rural Mexico are built of adobe, bricks made from mud and straw. In the warmest areas, straw roofs cover houses made of wood. Open doorways allow breezes to pass through the house. Shaded hammocks make a cool resting place for babies, children, and adults.

While small farms have changed very little over the years, the nearby villages have grown into cities. Poor people often leave their farms and come to the city looking for other kinds of work. They build shelters from found materials in areas without running water or electricity. Their lives are hard

Children in front of their country home

A house in the city

because there are not enough jobs. Mexico's government is trying to improve education and job opportunities for its poorest citizens.

Homes in Mexico's cities may be very different from one another. The families of those with good jobs live in modern apartment buildings or large, beautiful houses. Mexico's biggest cities bustle with schools, shops, restaurants, and movie theaters. They have all the problems of big cities, too: crowds, traffic jams, crime, and air pollution.

In many Mexican cities, the main streets look like the spokes of a wheel. They often lead to a town square called a *zócalo*. Government buildings, a church, hotels, restaurants, and movie theaters can be found there.

The busy streets of Mexico City.

Nearby is the *mercado* (market), a large, flat building with rows of stalls inside. In good weather, more stalls are set up outside. Vendors sell fresh meat, fish, fruits, and vegetables. Some offer handmade crafts. Others may bring the latest CDs or tennis shoes. Shoppers haggle over prices. If one vendor charges too much, another

A vendor sells silver jewelry.

can be found with a better price. Most cities have modern supermarkets as well, but shoppers still hunt for bargains at the *mercado*.

Family ties are important to Mexicans. Grandparents, aunts, uncles, and cousins often live near one another. After church on Sundays, they gather for the *comida*, a large mid-day meal.

Chicken with *mole* is a popular *comida* dish. *Mole* is a sauce made from dried peppers, chocolate, nuts, and spices. Some Mexican cooks like to keep their special *mole* recipes a secret. Tortillas are another favorite. They may be served alone—flat, hot, and steaming—or they may be used to create another dish called the enchilada.

Chili peppers add flavor and color to many Mexican dishes. There are more than one hundred varieties to choose from. Some Mexicans enjoy spicy foods, but others do not. Sauces, or salsa, made from chili peppers are served as side dishes. Each person uses as much as he or she likes.

After the *comida*, families often go to a park or the *zócalo*. There they can stroll, relax, and continue to enjoy the day together.

Tortillas for sale

Let's Eat!
Chocolate Mexicano

On cold mornings, Chocolate Mexicano is a favorite treat. The special Mexican chocolate used in this delicious drink is flavored with sugar and cinnamon. If you cannot find Mexican chocolate, you can use sweet cooking chocolate and add ground cinnamon. Brought to the table in an earthenware jug, Chocolate Mexicano is whipped until frothy with a wooden beater called a *molinillo*. You can use an egg-beater or wire whisk instead.

Ingredients:

6 ounces of
sweet cooking chocolate
(or two 3-ounce cakes of
Mexican chocolate)

6 cups of milk

1 ½ teaspoons of cinnamon
(use with sweet cooking
chocolate only)

Place all the ingredients into a saucepan and cook over low heat until the chocolate is melted. Stir constantly to blend—and to avoid burning. Beat until frothy just before serving. Serves four.

School Days

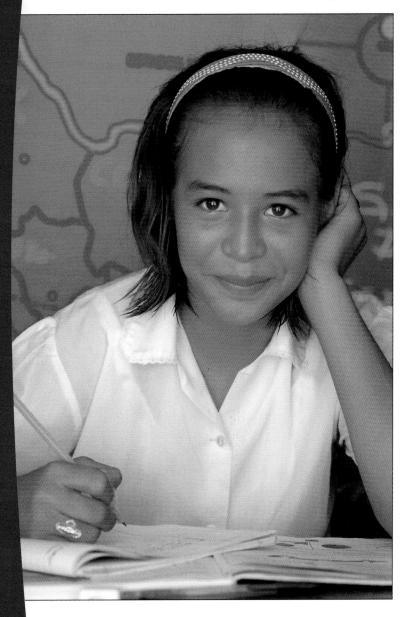

One hundred years ago, only 15 percent of Mexico's people knew how to read or write. There were very few public schools. Only the wealthiest families could afford to send their children to private schools.

After the Mexican Revolution ended in 1920, the government tried to build a school system for everyone. But it took many years for public education to reach the poorest people, who lived far from the cities on farms and in small villages.

Today, all Mexican children from ages six through fourteen must attend school. Some begin preschool before age six, and many others go on to high school and college.

There are three levels of public

At school in a small Mexican village

education in Mexico. *Primaria* (primary school) includes grades one through six. Grades seven, eight, and nine make up the *secundaria* (middle school). *Preparatoria* is very much like high school in the United States. The students with the best grades can apply to go to a university.

Students in Mexico usually wear uniforms to school. They attend classes five

Students in school uniforms

A school band rehearses outside.

days a week, Monday through Friday. In addition to weekends, they have time off for summer vacation and the Easter and Christmas holidays.

Mexican children study Spanish, math, science, history, geography, art, music, folk dancing, and physical education. They learn about their country's rich

Folk dancers in traditional dress

culture and the importance of protecting its land and animals. Some students also study English as a second language and log on to the Internet to learn about other countries.

In 1997, the Mexican government asked young people to help prepare a list of important rights for children. Millions responded, and most of them put the right to go to school at the top of that list.

But many children still drop out of school without finishing their educations. They have to go to work instead, to help their poor families buy food and clothing. However, the students who are able to stay in school take their studies seriously. They know that an education is the way to a good future for themselves and for their country.

Graduation day

Los Elefantes
(The Elephants)

School children in Mexico like to sing this funny counting song:

Un e-le-fan-te se ba-lan-

cea-ba so-bre la te-la de u-na a-

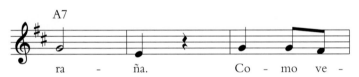
ra- ña. Co-mo ve-

í - a que re-sis-tí - a

fue-ron a lla-mar a o-tro e-le-fan - te.

¡Va-ya e-le-fan-ta-zo que se die - ron!

English:

An elephant stood on the web of a spider.
She thought it was strong; she thought
    she was lighter.
Along came a friend. She called to
    invite her.

Two elephants...
Three elephants...
Four elephants...
Five elephants...
Six elephants...

Seven elephants stood on the web of a
    spider.
They thought it was strong; they
    thought they were lighter.
The elephant's friends all fell down
    beside her.
Oh, no! What a mess on that web of a
    spider!

29

Just for Fun

In their free time, children in Mexico's cities enjoy watching television and movies and playing video games. Some belong to scout troops. Others study ballet or practice musical instruments after school.

Mild weather means that much of life in Mexico can be enjoyed outdoors. Restaurant walls roll wide open so that diners can eat outside. Vendors sell food and souvenirs on the street. Flowers bloom in courtyards. Shady parks and plazas welcome young and old.

Almost everyone in Mexico enjoys outdoor sports, and their favorite is *futbol*. That sounds like the

Handmade baskets for sale

American game of football, but it is actually soccer. There are school teams and professional leagues. Young people play *futbol* after school, too, wherever they can. In the desert, cactus plants may serve as goalposts!

A soccer fan enjoys an exciting game.

Young cowboys at a rodeo

Baseball is the country's second favorite sport. Mexico has sent many fine players to leagues in the United States and Canada. There are baseball diamonds in most city parks. Where the weather stays warm, baseball can be played year-round.

Boxing and bullfighting are very popular. The biggest bullfighting ring in the world is in Mexico City. Even the smallest towns put up rings and hang lights on their plazas to stage a boxing match or bullfight.

Rodeos are popular in northern Mexico. *Rodeo* is a Spanish word meaning round. Mexican cowboys used to form a circle around a group of cattle to separate them from the herd. Now, rodeos are a place to display many kinds of riding and roping skills.

Music is often enjoyed outdoors. Guitarists strum on park benches. Student groups sing on the plaza. *Mariachis* stroll the streets, playing for money. Local folk dancing groups also

Mariachis play for passersby.

perform on the plaza, dressed in their colorful native costumes. Along with folk music and dancing, Mexicans enjoy classical music, rock, jazz, opera, and ballet.

Mexicans and tourists alike explore the huge stone pyramids left by earlier Maya, Aztec, and other native civilizations. Some pyramids were used as temples for religious ceremonies. Others were burial tombs for ancient emperors.

Mexico's many beaches are a favorite of tourists, but Mexicans relax and play there as well. Children who live near the water learn to swim early. Acapulco on the west coast and Cancún in the east are famous vacation spots.

Indoors or out, there's always something to see and do in Mexico!

Floating among colorful fish and coral

Los Tres Toquecitos
(Three Gentle Raps)

This is a game for at least three players, or as many as want to join in! It is a lot like hide-and-seek, and can be played indoors or outside.

The player who is It is called the Porter. He stands beside a goal, called the Door. With his eyes shut, the Porter counts slowly to twenty. All the other players hide. Then the Porter opens his eyes and searches for them. But he always tries to stay close to the Door. At the same time, the others try to sneak closer to the Door without being seen by the Porter.

When the Porter sees a player, he must run to the Door, rap three times, and shout, "One, two, three for (the caught player)!"

But the other players are also trying to run to the Door so they can rap three times and say, "One, two, three for me!"

If a player is caught by the Porter before getting to the Door and rapping, that player becomes It. But if the player makes it to the Door and raps first, he becomes the Porter's helper.

Then the Porter and his helper search for others who are still hiding. Whoever spots another player first runs to the Door and shouts, "One, two, three for (the caught player)!" Then the caught player becomes the Porter.

But if the player is fast enough to get to the door and rap before the Porter or his helper, he or she is safe and becomes another helper for the Porter. Then all three search for the players who are still hiding.

In Spanish, say "¡Uno, dos, tres por mí!" (One, two, three for me!) or "¡Uno, dos, tres por (your friend)!"

Let's Celebrate!

Hardly a day goes by without a celebration somewhere in Mexico. In the largest cities and the smallest villages, people love to plan *fiestas*.

Birthdays call for family parties, but saints' days are even more important. Each saint in the Catholic Church has a feast day once a year. Everyone with that saint's name also celebrates on that day, often with a party for relatives and friends. Towns have patron saints, too. Yearly *fiestas* honor them with parades, fireworks, music, dancing, and lots of delicious food.

The country of Mexico also has a patron saint, Our Lady of Guadalupe. All of Mexico celebrates Guadalupe Day on December 12. Many Mexicans travel long distances to visit a church in Mexico City that was built in her honor.

Christmas celebrations begin in mid-December with a tradition called Las Posadas (Christmas Pageants). Candlelit processions wind through Mexican towns and cities. Children carry statues of Mary and Joseph. In some places, a girl dressed as Mary rides a donkey, while a boy dressed as Joseph walks beside her. House to house they go, singing a song that asks for a place to rest. At each

Lively folk music and dancing at a park

stop, children sing back, "Go away. There is no room."

Finally, one house welcomes them. Prayers are said, and it's time for a party. Refreshments are served. A clay or papier-mâché *piñata* is hung from the ceiling or from a tree limb out in the courtyard. Children take turns being blindfolded and swinging at the *piñata* with a stick. When someone finally breaks the *piñata*, small treats, such as fruit and nuts, pour out.

Posadas may go on in different neighborhoods for nine evenings. The last Posada, on Christmas Eve, ends at the local church, where prayers, songs, and dances often last all night long.

Christmas Day is quiet in Mexico—a day of rest after all the excitement of the Posadas. But the festive season continues through January 6, known as Día de Los Reyes Magos (Three Kings Day). This is when Mexican children receive their presents, in memory of the three wise men who brought gifts to the baby Jesus. Shoes are left by a door or window the night before, along with water for

A candy skull

A Cinco de Mayo parade

the camels carrying the three kings. In the morning, the water is gone and the shoes are filled with gifts.

El Día de los Muertos (The Day of the Dead) on November 2 is another important fiesta in Mexico. Weeks ahead, markets begin selling toy skeletons, skulls, and coffins. Children eat skulls made of candy. Graves are tidied and decorated with flowers. Families hold picnics in cemeteries, with the favorite foods of their dead relatives. El Día de los Muertos is a joyful celebration. By remembering loved ones, Mexicans know they too will always be loved and remembered.

Cinco de Mayo (The Fifth of May) is a festival celebrated in memory of the Battle of Puebla. On May 5, 1862, a small Mexican army joined forces with the citizens of the town of Puebla to defeat an invading French army. Today, parades and

Celebrating Independence Day

mock battles recall this important Mexican victory. Cinco de Mayo has also become a popular holiday in the United States.

Independence Day, or Dies y Seis de Septiembre (The Sixteenth of September), is Mexico's most important national holiday. It marks the beginning of Mexico's revolution against Spain. In 1810, a priest named Father Miguel Hidalgo y Costilla rang a church bell to rally the people to action. The war ended in 1821, and Mexico became an independent nation. Each year on September 16 church bells ring all over Mexico, and people echo Father Hidalgo's cry, "*¡Viva México!*" (Long live Mexico!)

Make a Mexican Piñata

You will need: a large balloon, white glue, a bowl, newspaper, two long pieces of string, a pin, masking tape, white paper, small candies or toys, and paint.

1. Tear the newspaper into strips about eight inches long and one inch wide.

2. Blow the balloon up and tie it shut.

3. Wrap the two strings around the balloon in two directions, as if you were tying ribbon around a gift box. Tie the strings in the center at the top of the balloon. Hang the balloon up by the strings where you can work on it easily.

4. Pour the glue into a large bowl and thin it with water until it is like cream.

5. Dip the strips of newspaper into the glue and press them onto the balloon, leaving a hole of about two inches around the knot. Keep adding strips of newspaper until the balloon is completely covered (except for that hole).

6. Continue gluing newspaper to the *piñata*. You'll need a total of about six layers. Then let it dry completely. This may take a day or more.

7. Holding the knot of the balloon, pop it with the pin. Gently pull out the balloon. Put the candies or toys into the open hole. Do not make the *piñata* too heavy!

8. Cover the hole with strips of masking tape. Then paint and decorate it.

9. Use the strings to hang the *piñata* for your party.

10. Blindfold players one at a time and take turns hitting the *piñata* with a stick. When it breaks, enjoy the treats!

There are three bars on the Mexican flag. The green stands for independence, the white represents religion, and the red means unity. The crest at the center shows a cactus growing out of a rock. An eagle stands on the cactus, holding a snake in its beak. According to legend, the Aztecs built their capital city of Tenochtitlán in a place where they saw this image. Mexico City now stands in the same spot.

The peso is Mexico's form of money. The exchange rate often changes, but currently one American dollar equals 9.08 pesos.

Count in Spanish

English	Spanish	Say it like this:
one	uno	OO-noh
two	dos	DOHS
three	tres	TRACE
four	cuatro	KWAH-troh
five	cinco	SEEN-koh
six	seis	SAYSS
seven	siete	see-EH-tay
eight	ocho	OH-choh
nine	nueve	NWEH-beh
ten	diez	dee-EHS

Glossary

Aztec   Native American civilization that once ruled much of Mexico.

enchilada (en-chee-LAH-dah)   Stuffed tortilla usually fried and covered with a sauce.

mariachi (mah-ree-AH-chee)   Traditional Mexican musician.

Maya (MY-yah)   Early civilization that was very advanced in mathematics and science.

molinillo (moh-lee-NEE-yoh)   Wooden stick used to whip hot chocolate into a froth.

peninsula (pen-IN-suh-lah)   Piece of land surrounded on three sides by water.

plateau (pla-TOH)   Large area of land raised higher than the land around it.

Rio Grande (REE-oh grahn-DAY)   River between the United States and Mexico.

tortilla (tor-TEE-yuh)   Round, thin pancake made of corn or wheat.

zócalo (SOH-cah-loh)   Central plaza in Mexican cities.

Proud to Be Mexican

Lola Álvarez Bravo (1907–1993)

Delores "Lola" Martínez de Anda was born in 1907 in the western province of Jalisco. Orphaned at the age of eight, she was raised by relatives. As a child, she admired the work of her neighbor and friend Manuel Álvarez Bravo, a photographer. She later married him and learned photography by working as his assistant. After a while, they took turns taking pictures with the same camera. For many years, Lola Álvarez Bravo photographed scenes from Mexico's culture and history for the National University of Mexico. Her wonderful photographs capture the beauty and spirit of Mexico and its people.

Adriana Fernández (1971–   )

At over 15,000 feet, Xinantecatl is the fourth highest peak in Mexico. This is where marathon runner Adriana Fernández trains for her races. She is one of several "volcano runners" who strengthen their lungs and muscles on the cold, rugged mountaintop. Born in Mexico City on March 4, 1971, Adriana started jogging at age fifteen, when she and her family decided to exercise more and lose weight. Four years later, she began running seriously, coached by Mexican champion Rodolfo Gómez. In 1995, she won the 5,000-meter race at the Pan American Games. Since then, she has set national records and represented Mexico in the Olympics and international competitions. In 1999, she won the women's division of the New York City Marathon.

Benito Pablo Juárez (1806–1872)

Benito Juárez was a Zapotec Indian. He was born to a poor farming family in Oaxaca on March 21, 1806. His parents died when he was only three. As a child, Juárez had to work instead of attending school. At the age of twelve, he left his village and traveled to Oaxaca City. There he lived with his sister and began his education. He went on to study law and become a judge. Later, he was elected governor of Oaxaca. As president of Mexico from 1858 until his death in 1872, Juárez fought hard for democracy, independence, and the rights of the poor.

Find Out More

Books

Children of the Yucatán by Frank Staub. Carolrhoda Books, Minnesota, 1996.

Food and Recipes of Mexico by Theresa M. Beatty. Rosen Publishing Group, New York, 1999.

Lost Temple of the Aztecs by Shelley Tanaka. Hyperion, New York, 2000.

Mexico: 40 Activities to Experience Mexico Past and Present by Susan Milord. Williamson Publishing, Vermont, 1999.

Web Sites

http://www.demon.co.uk/mexuk/meet_mex

An excellent site for information and photographs about Mexican culture, history, and daily life, plus music, games, crafts, and recipes.

http://www.elbalero.gob.mx/kids

Facts, games, news, and more, presented by the Mexican Embassy.

Videos

Go to **http://www.inside-mexico.com** for a wide variety of videos for the whole family, including *Fiesta!*, *Family Sunday*, *Mexican Youth Today*, and *El Mercado: Mexican Marketplace*. This site also features a newsletter and a catalog of music from Mexico.

Index

Page numbers for illustrations are in **boldface.**

About the Author

Sandy Asher is the author of many books, stories, poems, and plays for young people. She loves to travel and has visited schools from Anchorage, Alaska, to St. Petersburg, Florida. You can visit her Web page at:

http://mowrites4kids.drury.edu/authors/asher.